Best Wishes

Leon Newton

Psycho-Politics In Government

A Dramatic Dialogue

Publisher's Cataloging-in-Publication Data

Newton, Leon T.
Psycho-politics in government: a dramatic dialogue / Leon T. Newton
p. cm.
ISBN 0-915885-02-6
1. Dialogues, English. 2. United States—Politics and government—Drama. 3. Political corruption—Drama. 4. Power (Social sciences)—Drama. 5. Political science—Philosophy—Drama. 6. Political psychology—Drama. 7. Imaginary conversations. I. Title.
PS3564.E917.P79 1993
812.54—dc20 93-85663 [BCS-0009]
CIP

Psycho-Politics In Government

A Dramatic Dialogue

Leon Newton

DEDICATIONS

Amnesty International for their unceasing efforts in the fight for the rights, respect and dignity of each human being.

In remembrance of the Holocaust that it never be revisited on mankind. In the belief that mankind will concentrate on constructive efforts to help foster hope, love, faith, and good will among mankind. Governments will use their powers to enhance the quality of human life on this planet.

My parents Mozella and William Newton. Their love and wisdom helped me to understand self-worth and the meaning of a person's existence is not based on material possessions but strength of character and nobility of purpose.

NOTE TO READERS

In our "New World Order" any political state built on fear and suppression must fail. Life being as it is, the question men ask themselves is "How much more suffering and oppression must my people and I endure?" Have not men reached that high plane in life where they realize that what hurts one of us hurts all, and that no man will experience pure freedom until all men are free. Many men think that, because of that experience within their own individual realm, they are free, but are they?

In *Psycho-Politics In Government* I have tried to convey the thoughts and the feelings of the many who must live under the regime of suppression.

Whether it be done by one or many, choice or force, it does not matter, because it's in complete chaos with life.

Titus revealed his political philosophy when he told Veritas that, "The state is to be served. The state has the right to dictate to men what it thinks necessary in order to perpetuate itself, regardless of men's own convictions on ethical and moral questions."

"What is left of life, if all the things that encompass, enhance, and sustain life are taken from men? The world was not created by men, but was created for them. There are those who have forced others to mold and shape it to their own likings.

"Is this what I live for? The pleasure of other men?"

I should say not!

"The truth shall withstand all lies."

Many are called to defend the course of freedom, and the dignity of men, but only a few are chosen.

My only purpose for writing *Psycho-Politics In Government* is to preserve good government in the minds and hearts of the governed. Thereby producing *good* men to govern.

ACKNOWLEDGEMENTS

David G. Gil, professor of social policy at Brandeis University. Dr. Gil lectured at Harvard University as a visiting professor in the Extension Program.

While studying under him, he influenced my political philosophy considerably. Dr. Gil taught an evening course in analysis of social policy.

Barb N., Ringo and Ann Newton, who encouraged the completion of my book, who never lost faith in my ability to create or construct for the good of all.

The many friends at the University De Las Americas in Mexico, who examined my manuscript and offered their comments for improvement.

Eddie and Ray for suggested title change.

Dr. Choi, Dr. Perry, and Dr. Steward, my mentors at Marshall University.

PART I

Veritas stopped to rest under a tree. Suddenly, fifty armed guards immediately surrounded him. A tall, wrinkled man shouted, "Seize him!"

Veritas didn't move, his only reply to the Captain's command to his men, "Is it I you want?"

The Captain shouted, "What is your name?"

Veritas smiled, "I am called Veritas."

Captain, "The Emperor wishes that you be brought immediately to be convicted of trespassing."

Veritas, "I don't expect much better treatment from your Emperor Titus."

The Captain and his army seemed to have been perturbed that such an old man displayed courage in his captivity. One of the soldiers asked, "Could it be that this man called Veritas doesn't fear our Emperor Titus? For all those that come before him, it means death!"

Messenger boy, out of breath, "Emperor, Emperor! I have very important messages that have just arrived from various parts of your domains."

Titus, pensively, "Well, let's see what troubles you bring, boy, for if it is too bad a news, I shall have your head."

Messenger boy's face began to turn sad, "But, Emperor Titus, I am only the one who delivers the messages that I receive from the runners. I have no control over the destiny of men's lives."

Titus, greatly angered by the boy's words, "I have spoken, Guards, take this foul-mouth fool and cut his tongue out. It will serve as an example to all who must address themselves before me."

The boy begged and pleaded, but Titus just turned his head and walked away, while the boy was being dragged away shouting, "Emperor, Emperor! I beg of thee, have mercy!"

The Messages

Emperor Titus:

Beware of the stone man. For all I have to tell is to treat him with kindness. I beg of thee, don't accept the advice of the other Emperors. They have lost control of their domains and also wish you to join their fate.

I have seen this stone-faced man they call Veritas. He is powerful, and if he wishes, can cause great destruction. They say he has been sent by the gods. The gods or not, beware!

—Emperor
Tang of Plang

Emperor Titus:

Kill Veritas
Kill Veritas
Kill Veritas
before he destroys you.
They say he is of stone.
May fate be with you.

—Emperor Kong

Emperor Titus:

I write to you because it is of great importance. There is a stranger reported to be heading your way. They say he plans to enter you city. Arrest him for trespassing.

I saw his face turn into stone before my very eyes. NO man can lie before him. He is of truth. I believe the gods have sent him.

I am no longer Emperor of Chang, but am hiding out until the revolt is over. My life is in danger.

—A dear
and trusted friend,
Taingles

Emperor Titus:

For I must flee for my life, I have only a few words to leave you:

Stop Veritas! Stop Veritas!

—Emperor Sye

Emperor Titus:

Because we have fought many great battles together against our enemies, I must warn you of Veritas. He is very dangerous an not to be taken lightly.

He causes revolts and mass confusing. I too am a victim of his turmoil.

May the gods be with you.

—Emperor C. Kong

Emperor Titus:

Some men are fools, but you, Titus, must be wise. Flee your city while you are still alive! Leave, Titus, that you may live and rule again my brother.

Titus, Emperor Shaw has died at the hands of his revolting subjects. These are his last words to be sent to you.

—The High Priest,
Kang

Titus, pensively, "I dare that fool to think of entering my domain. My guards shall immediately arrest him. If the dog resists, my orders are to kill him. It would save me the trouble of judging this Veritas. No man comes before me innocent, for they are all guilty. Only the innocent do not come before me.

"I, Titus, have the power over life and death. I should have been born among the gods. If the gods have sent this Veritas, the stone-faced fool, it must prove that the gods are truly envious of me, the great Titus. The gods can only be envious of other gods. Could it be that I am one and not really aware of it?"

The Inquisition

Titus, "So you are the one who they call Veritas, who dares to enter my domain?"

Veritas, "I only journey through here on my pilgrimage."

Titus walks over and touches Veritas' face. "Tell me, Veritas, why do they call you the man with the stone face?"

Veritas, "What man knows and understands fully the folly of other men?"

Titus, "This may very well be your last pilgrimage. I am told you possess mystic powers. Show us where we might run like cowards."

Veritas, "Mockery is the first sign of a fool. It is said that the ways of an unjust ruler are like stray lambs entering a den of hungry wolves."

Titus, "You are not as wise as I thought. If only you knew what fate awaits you, that sharp tongue would halt! For you are surely a fool to speak such things to Titus the Great. By just a slight gesture of my hand, I can have your bones crushed as fine as flour. Your life means nothing to me."

Veritas, "I didn't come here to amuse you nor entertain, but only speak the things of which I know are true. So, Titus, you think of yourself as a God. It is written that all that a man isn't, he wishes. When men no longer strive for the betterment of self, they usually end up worse than they started. Life is not yours, Titus, to give or take. If you think of yourself as the sole giver and taker of life, tell me, Titus, who grants and denies you yours? I am told that your laws are Titus' laws. Laws by which no just man can expect or obtain justice."

Titus, "I believe that equity should only be granted to a select few. For all men claim to be just. They all come before me pleading they are innocent. If men had their own way, they would never allow themselves to be punished by the laws. Men are by nature rebellious. Rule or be ruled! The universe is not big enough to have such people in power."

Veritas, "What must this select few do to receive equity?"

Titus, "Remain loyal."

Veritas, "What are the qualities of your loyalists? Perhaps they think not in terms of good and evil, but what will only please Titus. For these are the kinds of men that perpetuate suppression. It appears you interpret laws not according to the gods, but one way, yours! Ruling fools and loyal liars are said to be of the same character. You must remember, Titus, that nothing from nothing leaves nothing. This is what the world thinks of foolish rulers and loyal liars. For you are dead and do not live. Life is to be lived, not just ruled.

"You and your loyal bureaucrats are thieves and robbers! This thievery is a tragedy because you rob not so much from their crops and earnings, but their lives. The hardship they must endure in their daily existence is known only among the dead. You have raped their bodies, and poisoned their minds."

Titus, "You speak all lies! What does a mere stranger know of the Great Titus' deeds and how he governs? What folklore have you heard of me? There are many who would like to see me dethroned or killed."

Veritas, "Titus, all do not lie. A man's vice is his defense against the truth. For he cannot use it as an instrument against evil. What little do you know of the forces operating for the good of men? You are not evil by nature, only by action and deeds. Power and the ability to govern are not evil in themselves. It's how one achieves power, what means you employ to reach your goal. How much vice can a man swim in and still be called a man? Some men are like wild animals who must be tamed. For them, government suits their purpose. According to you, Titus, there is nothing wrong with the way you govern. You have only to ask yourself, 'Would I live under the condition in which I rule others?' The answer must be sought from the heart, not the conscience. Men rationalize their vanity, but the heart doesn't compromise. Would I obey unjust laws issued by a fool-hearted Emperor? What price would I be wiling to pay for my people's freedom? For the price of freedom is high!

"To be ruled by a fool—I say it is better not to be ruled at all! When men contemplate freedom, they are truly the lovers of life. I say that to remain a slave is death and to become free is life. Without freedom, reality is distorted. You and your band of thieves have been fortunate in that your subjects have accepted themselves as subordinates and slaves of the state."

Titus, "I live not for the pleasure, nor the likings of other men."

Veritas, "You are right, Titus, but you force others to heed to yours."

Titus, upset with Veritas, "I am their Emperor! For I live only for Titus."

High Priest, who had been listening carefully, jumped up and walked over to Titus. "Not even for the gods? The gods must be obeyed. It is written that the gods shall have all preference over mortals. Whatever decision that Eros, our god of Law, delivers to me must be abided by.

Titus, you are the protector and guardian of the Sacred Law. The gods shall surely be angry."

Titus, raging, replied, "Let the gods rule their domain, and I shall rule mine!"

While the High Priest eagerly hurried away, Titus turned towards the other members of the deity who were sitting in the court and shouted, "You, all exist because I alone, Titus the Great, allow you. Do as I say or you will be soon taking orders from the gods."

Veritas, "Titus, you have accepted the job of the gods, but you refuse to use the wisdom and discretion only the gods have knowledge of. Your character isn't for ruling, but must be ruled. Laws are instituted to tame the many Tituses that would immediately seize power, at any expense."

Titus, "Maybe the things you speak interest me. I allow you to live a bit longer."

Veritas, "But for how long?"

Titus, "Excellent question."

Veritas, "The universe has been created for Titus alone."

Titus, "Hold your tongue or I will have it cut out, and forced down your throat."

Veritas, calmly, "Your threats don't disturb my soul. Your life is in my hands, not mine in yours."

Titus laughed, realizing Veritas was strapped to a chair surrounded by guards. "Now tell me, wise one, now that you imagine you have it. What do you plan to do with it?"

Veritas, "Every man shall be shown the path to enlightenment. Yes, Titus, even you. NO man knows what fate awaits him."

Titus, "Veritas, you are really good at riddles."

Titus, "I contend that all men are corrupt by nature.

My philosophy is that it is better to rule than to be ruled. Most men would rather give orders than take them, break laws rather than to obey. It's the nature of the political man to want to rule and seek power. When he finds it, he uses it, the best way he knows how.

"Power is for all, but all aren't powerful. I rule because it is my fate that I must rule. Power is a means by which one acquires and controls.

"It is only natural for me to love and want to maintain power. Power brings me the things death cannot. Without it I, like many other rulers, will cease to exist. Power is my life force.

"The struggle for power is that driving force which keeps me on top and everyone else on the bottom. As the Emperor from Kong says, 'Everyone else as slaves and me free.'

"I have often thought, if I had to become a slave, I would take my life. I would rather be dead than to exist as a slave.

"At night I don't sleep very well, probably because of those I had to condemn to death. I see their faces at night. Many of them are stained with blood. They scream at the top of their voices saying, 'Titus, Titus, why, why? Are we not men in your eyes? Why have you denied us the very thing you cling onto? Life! Life! Life!'

"For I have done nothing wrong. All I have condemned deserved nothing better than death. I haven't any regrets for those I have passed judgment on. They broke the law and were punished."

Veritas, "Mercy, love, and forgiveness are akin to the human spirit."

Titus, "I believe in only justice, mercy is a sign of a week Emperor. Pardons are granted by the gods in their domains, *not* Titus!"

Veritas, "Life doesn't evolve around power, but the good use of power. You are obsessed with power, but you can never possess power. You profess it but it denies you.

Titus, raging, "Enough of this fool talk. Guards, throw this disgusting beast in prison, in hopes that he will be devoured by the creatures that may inhabit there."

PRISON

"Death ceases existence in us.

While Life creates existence for us."

Veritas felt the cool air on his flesh. The dampness was throughout the cell. The only light that entered through the long narrow cracked walls were dim. Veritas breathed very slowly from the stale air.

While sitting in the corner contemplating the things which must come to pass, something suddenly moved, which resembled a human form. Veritas got up to see just what it was.

There lay a young man in his mid twenties, badly beaten. The young man looked up, "Who are you?"

Veritas, "I am Veritas."

Young man, "I am called Taing."

Veritas, "What crime have you committed?"

Taing, "Is life always full of questions? They say I am a thief. The administrators are the biggest thieves of them all. The laws have always treated the rich and poor different."

Veritas, "He who steals bread to satisfy his hunger is not a thief. A hungry man doesn't need more laws. A hungry man cares not for laws. Titus thinks when men are hungry his laws will satisfy their bellies. Why do men love laws more than themselves? Laws are protectors of men, but men are protecting laws. Are not the laws meant to serve men? Titus has men to serve laws. The laws are not always unjust.

"In order to ensure equity in man's existence, government can be used as a means for which the greater amount of freedom can be experienced by all.

"I have witnessed misery and suffering, among all people. They are all men, except the poor are ruled while the rich rule. The secrets of the universe will remain locked forever. Nevertheless, men will not cease trying."

Taing, "Why do you speak in riddles? Is not life confusing enough? Why cannot men be free, must there always be misery and suffering? I want to love life, but it has refused to love me."

Veritas, "If the world seems cruel to you, maybe it is revenge you seek and not love. Life is cruel at times, but must we also be cruel?"

Taing, "I have struggled and often wondered at times for what. Must men always struggle to exist?

"Tell me, Veritas, why do men go against their gods when they know what they are doing is wrong? Are they blind to truth?"

Veritas, "Men respect the wishes of mortals, complying to their wishes regardless of the vanity."

"Religion is only respected in theory. It is looked upon only as a code of conduct. Religion serves men when they think it's in their best interest. The difference can be explained in terms of present and the future. Men are impatient, they want their rewards now, not later. Religion promises good conduct will be rewarded, later."

Taing, "But why?"

Veritas, "Men believe in what they want. The truth isn't always beautiful. Painful sometimes as it is, it has to be accepted. Truth is the key to enlightenment."

Taing, "We talk as if we were old friends. Yet, you are

so strange."

Veritas, "Because I am strange to you, it must not be interpreted as a lack of my appreciation for life. The absurdity of life is not in that men are different but only in their minds. Deception does not inhabit the soul, but is in minds of men. From it men experience madness. Those who commit atrocities are mad."

Taing, "Death is near. I can feel its closeness. I know I must embrace it, but at times I feel I must let it go. If men seek death, what can be expected from life? Could death be an escape from life?"

Veritas, "You think to be free one must experience death. Men must look within themselves, if they are to experience the deepest meaning of freedom. No man can enslave the soul. Men must be free in order to live and love life and experience the fulfilled meaning of one's existence.

"Today and tomorrow promise nothing. One must live each and every day as if it's his last."

Taing, "Veritas, men are the only creatures who are cursed with the knowledge of death."

Veritas, "The social contract between government and its people hasn't been fulfilled."

Taing, "I hear the guards approaching. Tomorrow is our trial."

Veritas, "My dear friend Taing, be not afraid of the things one expects and knows of. For you know sooner or later we must all face the inevitable. This is something every man would love to put off.

"There are men willing to prolong their lives, while denying others that right. There are many who give up their lives that others may live. There are those who are seekers beyond the realm of life and death. For they think that what they couldn't find in this world they will find in another.

"If you have refused to see or accept what life has to offer, what makes a man think that his soul shall be satisfied in another world?

"When leaders are corrupted by their blind greed and lust for power to prevail upon the minds, hearts, and soul of their people, the state suffers. Government must no longer be blinded by its hidden political agendas. Government's most valuable resource is not gold or silver, but the human spirit, if only government would use its power to harness that resource rather than wasting time, money, and energy in producing things which destroy life rather than create life. Leaders are entrusted with the power of government, which is only power to do the will of the people."

The Revelation

"Under suppression can a man misuse and abuse others, and still be rightfully called a man? I should say not! Even among the wildest beast there is compassion. For a man to destroy life in his efforts to gain power is mad."

—Veritas

Titus, "I, your Emperor, have brought two men to be judged by you. Taing is a mere thief. This one they call Veritas, beware of him. He speaks with a sharp tongue. I shall let you judge this liar, the master of deceit. He says you are all fools, incapable of rational judgments. Speak, Veritas, now, because after you finish, death you will know."

The clouds started to move, blocking out the sun. The crowd had moved closer together, some were very afraid. Never before had they seen such a man look towards the sky, while his body turned to stone. Titus couldn't believe what he saw. He walked over to touch the tall lifeless body. Taing, who had been standing next to Veritas, also moved slightly away. The executioner ran from the platform into the crowd. Someone in the crowd asked, "Is he alive?"

"Yes," responded an old man. "He was sent from the gods."

"No, he is evil," said a woman.

"Titus, Titus, save us from this thing," shouted the

crowd.

Titus, "What can I do to this figure of stone?"

Just as Titus turned and began to walk away, a voice shouted out, "Titus, you shall not go. Today, you shall be judged." Titus attempted to run, but his body stood at a standstill.

The crowd was very much impressed with his power.

Titus, "Quickly, destroy him," but the guards were too frightened to move.

"Listen to him not. He comes before you to speak lies against me, your Emperor. I have done much for you, surely you will not let a stranger who is evil possess you. I command you to destroy him!"

The crowd said nothing.

Veritas, "I come not to enslave you, but to free you from the chains of death.

"There are fools who allow other fools to reign over them. The reason Titus reigns is because you see in him some kind of mystic, God-like power, that only immortals possess. This deceptive concept that only a few are destined to lead while the others must follow is false. For those of you who have, there is no other course, but to be content with your plight. Apathy will not produce constructive results.

"Will a sane man ask a blind man for direction? Why as a people do you remain blind to these self-centered, egotistic lovers of power and money? They determine your fate and your children's.

"Is it 'just' for you and your children to have to suffer at the hands of these political fools? If you will not fight for justice and domestic reforms, who will? Or will a select few take on the battle?

"Too often, reforms have a hidden self-interest, supported and imposed on the masses, but only benefit a few.

"If the battle is fought to obtain freedom, and lost, the battle was never fought. Because the battle for freedom is a fight to the finish. Either you will emerge as the victors or the victims. The battle in time is inevitable. It is destined to be fought. Without freedom, there can be no life worth living.

"There has to be a certain degree of freedom if life is to continue. One must find something in life worth living for, and freedom is part of it. Freedom must never become out of men's reach or word, only the angels whisper about experiencing. If freedom in life you value, then it must be worth fighting for!

"The cowards run, and say, 'For we are weak. What can we do?' While the warriors say, 'What can be worse than suppression?'

"I say it is better to 'live in hell' than live under its rule! The population of a suppressed state is inhabited by a few idols, who think they enjoy the pleasures of the gods.

"For it is not true that all of you are unjust and worship Titus, who set himself up as a God and cannot see through his pompous authority. For all its inhabitants are not fools or fooled by him. LIfe is a continuation of revelations of truism, something that any government based on suppression cannot tolerate. For truism is the key to the path for those of you who long to be free. By enlightenment I mean the perception and recognition of reality. The deplorable conditions you are living in are not the natural state for men, for Titus has psyched you into believing you have been condemned and doomed.

"Only fools rule other fools. How could you allow a man such as Titus, and his band of thieves, to rule your lives? What has Titus to offer you? Nothing but *hard times* and *unbelievable hell!*

"Why cannot all men be free, must there always be those who aren't? Why must men be captured like wild animals to be caged and trained for the use of others? Do men look upon life as such? They are only playing the part of hunter and the hunted. If this is the game men must play, they will remain there. For the laws are written for the jungle, not men. In this jungle, man has the mind of a fox and the courage of a lion. Instead of emerging as the fox and the lion, men have been transformed into wild beasts and liars, in their attempt to maintain the perpetuation of their power. For they believe, like Titus, that power is desired by all, and that he who obtains it must rule all.

"You are told by Titus that you have little control over your fate, because the gods influenced certain aspects of it. Between the gods and Titus' bands of thieves, what is left for you to rule? Have you lived your existence in vain if you don't control and direct it? Either you will learn to mold and shape your lives, or others will!

"There will always be men swimming in a lustful pool of power. Titus thinks there is something holy about being able to command men to act against their will. Some men shall always seek its mystic powers.

"No state under the reign of suppression can expect its people to be happy, while a few flourish and the masses are experiencing misery and poverty.

"No man has been ordained by the gods where only a few are born to rule and others must obey. Men have been entrusted with the power *not* to rule but to solve the problems of government, to help administer justice throughout their domain as well as dealing with the problems with aid from their administrators.

"A ruler must rule because it is by choice, not force.

An apathetic people will remain under rule of suppression. Freedom and not apathy is what preserves life as well as enhances it. How can you tell others about the sweetness of life, if all you taste is bitterness? You do not know of the things you haven't experienced.

"Suppression breeds violence and revolutions. What comes out of revolution depends on the motives. Short-term goals are much more desirable during the planning stages of the revolution, because a criterion can easily be developed, as a means by which one can evaluate his progress. From this it can be determined whether or not one is successful in reaching the stated objectives. This allows more attention being concentrated on the long-range objectives. Nevertheless, the success of the revolution depends on the ability to focus on its entirety.

"If the revolution isn't successful, those who have potential to become leaders will remain followers. Is there any among you who dare think not as Titus, or the state? Thinking is dangerous, especially when you no longer accept your fate as a way of life.

"When the optimist begins to replace the pessimist, what else is there for the pessimist to do but get out? Man must not always expect the worst but always hope for the best. The subjects are only as good as the ruler. If your ruler is unjust, how can you expect to obtain justice from Titus, when he himself refuses to be just? Yet Titus expects it from his subjects and death is waiting for all those who are not.

"Titus hasn't set any examples for those to admire or follow. One can even learn from the ways of a fool. How long will a fool rule? It will depend on how long his subjects feel powerless to accept change.

"There are those who know no other way of life but to exist and be content, while under the leadership of a beast. Even among the beasts there is compassion. How can a man rule if he cannot rule his own household? Nevertheless, these are the men in power rather by choice or not. For they are the masters of deceit. They promise everything but deliver nothing. They are talking loud and saying nothing.

"Why cannot men be free? Slavery was never meant for men, and must never be accepted as a part of their existence. For those who practice it are mad. It's one of the most insane acts forced upon men. Yet, men have rationalized it for sanity. For many of you help Titus to perpetuate his rule of oppression so that you may obtain his favor, to experience freedom only for yourselves.

"The ways of rulers of suppressed states are illegal and illicit. They conjure plans to diminish the elements and forces operating to sustain life.

"How can man commit atrocities under suppression and still demand to be called a man? Even the title 'beast' is too kind for such a creature. Leaders must face the realization of life and its existence while reigning.

"The thing we don't like to talk about is called death. Yes, death claims us all, even the ruling tyrants! How will they plead and bargain when death knocks at their door? Will they scream and beg, or accept it, like those whom they have condemned unjustly? They will be held for the lives they have denied and taken for the atrocities they helped execute. Will they accept full responsibility?

"Your ruler, Titus, is a non-thinker, in that he lacks insight into how to elevate his subjects. The insight he has is how to elevate himself and the state from the sweat and toil of his subjects. At your expense, he will do anything. For Titus loves Titus and no one else! Titus lives for Titus and no one else!

"The nearest thing man can imagine to hell is to live

under the regime of suppression; for suppression is hell itself—the burning hot flames which slowly burn away life.

"Why must men be fools? Will men think for themselves? Are rulers born, or did time and change happen to them all? Why do some men rule and others do not? Any man who has to rule by force to maintain his position deserves it not. He is mad to stay there for he is hated by all, mad because he is unwilling to admit his imperfectness. One who rules with blood in mind doesn't take his own life too seriously. They are easily obsessed with the idea of dominance over others.

"Power can be used as an instrument for the improvement in man's life. Power is only a force operating in the universe that a few attempt to use for the good of all. Is it necessary that man's true nature has to be suppressed? Could it be that we ourselves would use, and abuse, power, that we believe no one would pursue truism? Surely, all men are not corrupt, are they?

"Confused thinking, conflicting opinions and irrational impulses—neurotic behavior can never be justified when it leads to the death of men. Loyalists always proclaim their tyrant is doing the job well, for they are loyal fools who are blind and refuse to see the evil he conjures. They carry out their administrative duties with their eyes closed, and fingers in their ears. To remain in their position, they must act and not think. I have only one question for Titus' thieving bureaucrats: 'Where is your conscience?' Lying, cheating and stealing are all that rulers know under suppression. For they are all mad!

"A government at its worst is reflected by its corruption and poverty. When its people have worked from sunup to sundown that they may have something to show for their labor, no government has the right to demand more, when there isn't any more to be demanded. The state values its people only in terms of their ability to produce. When the years creep up on them, they are immediately regarded as worthless creatures. You must not only merely exist in life, but live life. Consciously, many of you worship the state and Titus. Many of you are born to serve and die for the state.

"Under suppression, man is in a state of confusion. He doesn't know whether life is death or death is life. When men began to contemplate their existence, they also focused on the forces in the universe which influence their existence. The most worthless ruler is the one who rules under suppression. He would rather rule others than himself. He delights in the subservience of others, of all the lives he has denied. Death is too good as a redress. When a man lives under suppression, his soul is never at rest. For many, death is a recourse, they would rather seek death than be slaves. For they think if freedom can be experienced through death *so shall it be!*

"Be aware of the ruler who has to fight like hell to obtain and maintain his power. So you will surely experience pure hell in your efforts to remove him.

"Aloofness causes dissension which causes strife. Men were not born in chains. It is by reason alone that they should not die in chains."

Listening to Veritas were a group of Sophists who had roamed into the city.

Sophist I, "I have listened well to much of what you said. You speak much truth, but tell me, where do you come from? Are you not a god? Why have you turned yourself into stone? What have you done to the one called Titus? Why cannot he move?"

Veritas, "For there are many things in the universe which shall remain a mystery to men."

Sophist II, "I listen not to what a man says but judge him only by his deeds. Tell me, Veritas, what deeds may I judge you by?"

Sophist III, "Men need to belong to some clan or group. Without it he feels lost and alone. The state provides protection for him from others who may try to destroy their clan, if men band together under one rule and allow the state to take care of their needs. Is it better?

"To be ruled by one than many in a state where there is absolute control, its subjects enjoy the greater amount of freedom. They don't have the burdens of thinking of their existence. It is determined for them. They can concentrate on other affairs of the state. The state is life; it helps sustain life, not deny life, Veritas, as you say. Without the state, men would cease to exist. The state must rule, not men, if there is to be unity."

Veritas, "No state is above men. The state must always come second to the needs of men. For without men, there would be no state. How can the creation be valued more than the creator? No man can justify the absolute control over life. The dignity is in man and not the state. When the state has been set above men, enmity is the only recourse that will lead to extreme wickedness and monstrous offenses. Men in a desperate attempt to claim their noble position will not laugh."

Sophist I, "Veritas, do you think it is wrong to want to rule?"

Veritas, "No! but only when men have gone mad, and are obsessed with power to the point where they no longer care about operating under agreed codes of ethics, when justice isn't ensured or obtainable, when the laws are written in blood, and death to all who dissent, when altruism is no longer an essential part of one's disposition.

"It has been said that the love of money is the root of all evil; but I will tell you, the love of power is the source of all vice."

Sophist II, "Veritas, don't you know that money hasn't any power of its own, but the secret is what it can purchase?"

Veritas, "Yes, that is true. You, my Sophist friends, are skilled in the devious art of dialectics. There are those who are foolish and shall remain. There are those who think they are wise, but are the truest fools. There are those who strive to become wiser for they are truly wise. When reality is no longer satisfactory, men possess the need to create an illusion."

Before leaving, one of the oldest Sophists asked if Veritas would join them.

Sophist, "Veritas, our friend, come, join us in order that we may learn from you the things that no man knows except you. Please, won't you come and journey the path for truth?"

Veritas, "For the things which you seek I have found. The path you travel I have journeyed. These are the things each and every man must journey. I must warn you Sophists that many of the things you seek must be sought beyond life. Many have searched, but only a few souls have been satisfied."

Sophist III, "Truly, you are a great teacher. I know who you are—a philosopher of life, one who delivers a message from life, for life. Every age produces such a man. What I don't understand or can explain is that gift of turning oneself to stone.

"We have much traveling to do. Bye, Veritas, our friend. May we meet again."

Titus, "Tell me, Veritas, I am unable to move. What shall you do with me?"

Veritas, "It is not for me to judge you, just to reveal the truth. Do you fear death?"

Titus, "For death is inevitable."

Veritas, "Is that what you told those that came before you, even though you have practiced cynicism, deceit, hypocrisy and perjury, in order that you may maintain political control. For many it is considered unnecessary and totally inexcusable."

Titus, "A man who speaks many things, such as justice and law, you have not been trained in the art. Have you not any respect for the law?"

Veritas, "How dare you talk of respect for the law, when your own self-appointed administrators do not respect it? They drag in the poor before the courts and fine them beyond their ability to pay. The poor are the victims of the law. They can only receive justice for a price. For you jails are full of them who cannot pay.

"Jails were never built for the rich, only the poor, those who have been denied access to full equality in all life endeavors. Because the state has failed to provide the essentials to sustain life, the victims of the law are all those who must struggle from day to day in order to exist. For this they must pay the price with their lives.

"Laws have been instituted for the protection of men, but who shall protect men against the unjust laws?"

Titus, realizing that he was now free to move, turned around, stepped back from the crowd into the courtyard, where the deity had been standing around listening to Titus.

Veritas, "Yes, Titus, you are you and I am I. For that is the difference!"

Titus, "I would rather be me than you, Veritas."

Veritas, "Titus, from life philosophy the knowledge I have gained I do not regret, but love. Truth should be pursued more often among all men. When truth is no longer pursued, what is the worth of a man?

The High Priest walked over to the platform next to Veritas.

High Priest, "This man who has turned to stone, they call him Veritas. Taing is nothing more than a mere thief. For death they do not deserve. Yet, as little as you know of this man, you despise him and want to steal his life.

"Let's consider your condition before Veritas entered our state. Many of you were slaves. Hunger haunted your friends and family. There were no laws and no order. Justice was nowhere to be found. Equity and men being treated like men were not to be heard. Philosophy and the classics were abolished and forbidden. Oppression you learned to live with and accept. Because many of you have suffered so much from Titus' reign, you became acquainted with death, for you feared it not!

"Veritas believes in one god and we in many. Veritas' god is from the East, ours from the West. Titus has gone mad! He no longer obeys the gods. He has cursed the gods and denounced them. He refuses to rule not from the gods' legal doctrines, but Titus'! He thinks of himself as a god. He enjoys the pleasures that only the gods are entitled to. The gods are angry, and because of this you all must pay for allowing Titus to rule. Today Titus has ruled his last. For you are guilty, even death is against you.

"We deserve all that the gods impose upon us. How could we allow ourselves to be ruled by a beast? Even *we* are told we must forgive. We shall never forget.

"Go now, Titus, before we turn to beasts and devour your soul. Go live among the beasts like yourself. You have proven that you cannot live among men, nor they with you. We do not thirst for your blood, as you did for ours. Many of us were too frightened to challenge you. Now we have nothing to lose. We have lost most of the people and things which were dearest to us.

"Get out of our sight, you creature from the darkness.

"For worshipping him, you must be punished. I deliver only the message the gods sent. You all must experience severe labor. The state shall be hit with plagues, famines and extreme poverty."

An old woman asked, "How long will the gods punish us?"

High Priest, "As long as they think sufficient."

After hearing this, the crowd turned to Titus.

Crowd, "Titus, haven't we suffered enough? Some of us have paid with our lives. Death is too good for you, Titus. If the dead you condemned unjustly returned, we wonder what possible punishment they would impose on you."

Titus, running out of the city, shouted back, "You ungrateful dogs. For what do you know? You are only men who must be ruled."

Veritas, "When leaders are corrupt, and betray the public trust, their nation suffers, worse yet its people.

As long as there is God, there is always hope.

"My friend, Taing, forsakes thee and began to live. It is better to be free than to remain in jail. I asked them to pardon you of your crime. A liar and a thief the world hates, be wise and take heed. I must go, but may truth and freedom remain with you always."

Part II

The Death of Titus

"Every man sooner or later must face himself."

—Veritas

Man's inhumanity to man must not be so commonplace that such acts do not stir in us indignation to end such acts.

Veritas was passing a bush in the forest when he heard someone experiencing great pain. There was Titus lying in a pool of blood. Two daggers were plunged into his body—one in each side of his ribs. The golden daggers had the words inscribed on them, "For the Love of Titus."

Veritas carefully removed the daggers from Titus' ribs.

Titus, "go, for fate has called and I must answer. Because of you, Veritas, I must share this fate."

Veritas, "You planned your own fate, while ruling and causing much misery."

Titus, "Tell me, Veritas. Why do you help such a man like me? When I left the city, there were some men who followed me out. After reaching the forest, they attacked me as if I were a threat to their lives."

Veritas, "You were once! Men may forgive, but they don't easily forget. I help you, Titus, because you are a man. What you have done doesn't concern me while you are hurt and near death."

Titus, "Are you any different than most men? Men are natural lovers of themselves.

Veritas, "What good have you known, Titus, to come

from wars? How can men elevate war, that which denies life, rather than saves it? It can never be justified regardless of the gains. It is better not to have gain than to profit from the lives of others. The price of man is priceless, but there remain many who will sell cheap. Then there are those who think only their lives are priceless, while others are worthless.

"How much a man values himself is in his own state of mind. It's not good for a man to think too much of himself. He must always search for balance."

Titus, "I fear death."

Veritas, "Why?"

Titus, "Because of what awaits me."

Veritas, "The conscience of a man will make him a coward, when fate comes and death is near."

Titus, "Oh, how I hate life!"

Veritas, "For many this is the only path to enlightenment. The absurdity of life is not when men think, but when they do not."

Titus, "The ugliness of life is tumult in the human dilemma, and I was a participant. Why must death approach all before we appreciate life? Men have courage, but death takes their dignity.

"I ask, veritas, can a man die proud? Why cannot men cry? For I am filled with sorrow and great pain, but yet I cannot allow it to escape."

Veritas, "Titus, if you feel like crying, cry! Men think they must carry the world on their shoulders. When men cease to release emotion, they are no longer men, but gods of perfection."

Veritas knew that Titus was becoming weaker. Veritas took his hand and placed it over Titus's heart.

In a weak voice, Titus said, "Veritas, I have done no wrong."

Titus looked up at Veritas and smiled and slowly closed his eyes as he clenched his fists. His body was cold just as he ruled.

Holding Titus' lifeless body in his arms, Veritas thought, "Men will always be men. For men in their folly will always convince themselves they have committed no wrong."

"How can a man love so little of his life? Life will not cease because of men."

For the love of life is life.

Sincerely written *From Life—for Life*

—Leon Newton

"The creator has given us souls equal to all the world, and yet satiable not even with a world. Everything is possible to man. Time can remake all things. We shall perhaps at last learn the noblest lesson of all, that man must not fight man, but must wage war only on the obstacles that nature offers to the triumph of man."

—Francis Bacon

Other books forthcoming by the author:

The Social Contract in Modern Political Thought

The Social, Economic and Political Planners of the New Society

Natural Jurisprudence and the State of War

An Essay on Biological Man

A Treatise on the Creative Artist

The Newspaper Boy

The Duel

The Village Poet

In Search of this One They Call God

Trying to Find Your Mind While Alone Losing It

Isaiah and the Hermit

A Day in Life

The Dismantlement of Antiquated Institutions of Nation States

ISBN 0-915885-03-4

PSYCHO-POLITICS IN GOVERNMENT

THE PLAY

LEON NEWTON

PSYCHO-POLITICS IN GOVERNMENT is a unique play that depicts how total trust in one person can induce a state of vulnerability, deception, and violence.

The Play centers around the righteous Emperor Titus and the evil actions of his power-hungry Chief Administrator named Creon. Creon coerces a guard to join him in his plans to assassinate the Emperor but the Emperor's son Damaus is able to see through Creon's false servitude and tries to warn his father. Because the Emperor is blinded by his faith in Creon, he is easily taken advantage of.

When Creon's assassination attempt fails, he blames Damaus for plotting the murder. When Titus ignores the pleas of his son, Damaus kills himself. Titus later learns, through the help of Veritas, a wise man with mystical powers, that Creon is the real villain. Titus's anger causes him to kill both Creon and the guard while Nemesis, the goddess of revenge, attempts to vindicate Damaus's name. Titus takes his own life but before he dies, Veritas has a serious discussion with Titus, trying to make him realize the folly of his ignorant ways. The tragic ending reveals man's weakness, fears, and selfishness.

PRODUCTION NOTES

All the action takes place inside the palace. There is only one set constructed. Act Two calls for special lighting effects.

Special effects are the use of colored lighting to give the effect something is going to happen. This can be done by dimming the lights and a smoke machine. Flashing lights off centered on Veritas can signify his transformation.

No. of Acts:	Two
Type of Drama	Tragedy
Number in Cast:	Three women and nine men
Number of Scenes	Five (no set changes)

THEATRICAL VERSION